THE #1

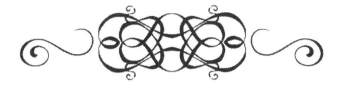

IMAGE MAKER

THE GUIDE INTO YOUR TRUE IDENTITY

IN HIGH DEFINITION

KEITH E. ECHOLS

FOR THOSE WHO CHOOSE TO BE UNSTOPPABLE

The Living Bible copyright © 1971 by Tyndale House Foundation. Used by permission of Tyndale House Publishers Inc., Carol Stream, Illinois 60188. All rights reserved. The Living Bible, TLB, and the The Living Bible logo are registered trademarks of Tyndale House Publishers.

This book is a work of non-fiction. Unless otherwise noted, the author and the publisher make no explicit guarantees as to the accuracy of the information contained in this book and in some cases, names of people and places have been altered to protect their privacy.

WestBow Press books may be ordered through booksellers or by contacting:

WestBow Press
A Division of Thomas Nelson & Zondervan
1663 Liberty Drive
Bloomington, IN 47403
www.westbowpress.com
1 (866) 928-1240

ISBN: 978-1-9736-0603-1 (sc)
ISBN: 978-1-9736-0601-7 (e)

Library of Congress Control Number: 2017916595

Print information available on the last page.

WestBow Press rev. date: 01/18/2018

DEDICATION

First and foremost, to my beloved teacher, my mother.

She put me on a never ending quest for wisdom and love. When I was five years old, I remember my mother using simple illustrations to teach me and my siblings the do's and don'ts of life.

For example, she wouldn't only say, "don't smoke cigarettes," she would say, "look at that chimney over there, see how it is smoking, things like that should smoke, not people."

Second, to my beautiful and gifted family, Alice and our four extraordinary children, Khalia, Sophia, Carmel and Joel. I love you very much for all your love and support.

Third, to my wonderful family and friends in Chicago, Los Angeles and New York, you're love is a phone call away and I treasure all of you.

FIRST WORD

It's not always automatic that we place ourselves at the top of our own priority list. At different times in our lives, we may not like ourselves very much. Even if we try to hide it behind a mask of smiles, the things you do and the words you say, will always show people just who you really are.

So if you estimate yourself not to be very important or if you think of yourself to proudly above others. This book is written for you.

I was in my early twenties and high school was a distant memory, my college days were also starting to vanish like a town in the rear view mirror of my mind. I was in the fast lane towards the many life changing decisions I was making and I needed help.

As you read this book and receive its message, you will be moved into a limitless and powerful view of life's possibilities.

The invisible world became visible and I went through a transformation that I am excited to share with you.

Growing up in a big city, I was constantly told to work hard, be smart and make a good living.

Working hard and smart for a good living is a very important part of life's pursuits.

However, like most young people at my age, life was happening to me. I wasn't really in control and didn't have a clue as to why certain things came my way. This was quite overwhelming.

But because of my mother's seeds of wisdom, I was determined to do life right and not stay in the darkness of ignorance.

My mother's strong advice was, "If you really are a good person and bad things happen to you, take a look in the Good Book and see if you fit." This changed me forever.

PREFACE

I call the message in this book a dive into the truth. Some people prefer to stick only their feet into the pool, or wade in the shallow waters of the truth, as it were.

However, divine truth is so very powerful and life changing, that we must dive in head first and totally submerge ourselves in it to be made free. Free from ignorance, free from foolishness, free from mental blindness and free from anything that produces lack of character.

Don't be the one who stands back and declares, "I don't like to think about deep things, especially the deep things of God and life." My question to that is "Why Not?"

Stay open and willing to learn. I also didn't know but I was open and I learned.

This book will give simple and basic teachings, views and real life stories, so that you will be able to recognize the hidden limiting thought patterns that maybe holding you captive from discovering your life's purpose. And robbing you of your peace of mind.

All too often, young adults are being grossly misled and seduced by materialism, selfish ambition, false religion and even scientific confusion.

It is time to be powerful, to arise, and to shine like the sun. Not to be bogged down by stress, addictions, mental confusion, no sense of direction or reason for living.

Now is the time! Because gross darkness is covering people.

INTRODUCTION

There are multitudes of images that are put before us daily. Even kids as young as eight years old are closely following trends, styles, and images promoted by Wall Street and Hollywood. Through TV, movies, magazines, music entertainment and social media.

Celebrities and entertainers try to have identifiable images that help to define and showcase their success. Sadly the problem is they are putting more emphasis on branding and packaging rather than integrity and character.

People seek acceptance from people who they want to imitate and look up to, as if it's a badge of honor. What people are you imitating? What crowds?

Is it the tattoos, body piercings, hip hop, geek-nerd crowd or high fashion, which one?

No matter what or with whom you identify, life is more important to limit and define yourself with just lifestyle and looks.

Who am I?
What am I here for?
What am I made of? That is the real deal!

Do I have responsibilities and values to go along with what I am trying to portray, or am I just trying to fit in?

Without the foundation of purpose, words such as shallow, superficial, selfish, hard hearted, proud and even emptiness will instead surround you.

There is a silent yet not so silent cry of a hurting generation, drowning their pain in music, sex, drugs and entertainment but does this really help?

None of those things should define you or define what is hidden beneath your exterior, deep down inside of you where your value and worth lies.

I am addressing the heart of the matter in this book.

The Image Maker is the one who made the big picture, the world, and then designed you and I to fit into it.

You are unique, like no other; there is great significance and power in you. Beyond your clothing and body, you are who God says you are! When you embrace the truth.

Just as the moon reflects the sun, humanity was designed to reflect the awesome light of our maker's goodness. Just as a child's looks and actions are similar to that of their parents. Humans were to reflect the love, power and greatness of the unseen architect of this vast universe.

Humans are not animals, even though some may act like cats and dogs. People were fashioned to be far better and greater than what some portray.

"So how do I change this?" You might ask.

"How do I get the help I need?"

If you are smart enough to take your car to the shop for repairs, and your unhealthy body to the doctor. Then I know you are smart enough to get the answers you need from this book.

So let's eat from the tree of wisdom together to discover our divine destinies and the point of our existence.

If that's not what it's all about, then what on earth are we here for? That is the big question. It is time to experience the transformation.

An image makeover of the divine kind. Earth is only the starting place, the school if you will, before eternity.

The world sees people as only consumers, promoting its ever degrading images and products because people are only concerned with making lots of money. We are much more valuable than mere consumers caught up in the latest fads and trends.

There are priceless gifts, talents and abilities given to each of us at birth to share with the world, showcasing us as the unique people we are designed to be. A beautiful tree with powerful life giving fruit to give to each other. We are to be producers, not just consumers. You are a treasure to be discovered. This is why we need parents, teachers, mentors and the Lord, to help us uncover our own treasure.

When humanity is God centered, we become greater than ourselves. God helps us experience the power for higher goals and plans, bigger visions and dreams. Your life will take on a new meaning with great satisfaction.

I believe as we get back to the original purpose of our being here, in line with God's plan, a brand new world will be awaiting us.

So, as you study the pages of this book and its message, you will receive jolts of inspiration to help move you to the highest level of life.

CONTENTS

Chapter

Chapter 1

EVERYBODY HAS POWER

From the top of a high mountain, the view is clear. But the view will change depending from what side of the mountain you are looking. An aerial view, however is an overall view and it can be vast. From this vantage point you will be able to see the rocky roads, dangerous areas and smooth places.

Let's take a look at the natural gifts and abilities, that humans possess from the sky view, and I call these things our power. These capabilities help us, show case the image of who we are.

In the beginning of time, it is written in Genesis 1 that a source of power beyond humankind formed, shaped and created everything that exists, both seen and unseen. That source is God, the Supreme Being.

Because of man's ruler ship over the earth, animals and nature, I believe that humans were built with and from power.

So how is this invisible power seen? Let's pause here to define what I mean by power.

Power is dominion, authority, force, intellect, energy, might, and influence, just to name a few. These words depict various ways in which power is seen or displayed.

1. Dominion is power to rule over a system or people. Power that directs or supervises that which dominates a circumstance.
2. Authority is the power at work within governments, kingdoms, military or police force, court systems, social and spiritual order all by legal rights or force of arms.
3. Influence is power to affect, impress, shape, motivate, persuade, inspire and to make someone or something significant.
4. Energy is power which creates motion, activity, vigor, drive, strength, passion, favor, charisma, just to name a few.

These powers are at work in the visible and invisible world. They are natural and supernatural.

In the miracle book the Holy Bible it is written, "Everything comes from God alone and everything lives by His power and everything is for His glory." (Romans 11:36) (TLB) Also, it says "He has no needs for He himself gives life and breath to everything, and satisfies every need there is." (Acts 19:25) (TLB)

He is not far from anyone of us. "For in Him we live and move and have our being." (Acts 17:28) (TLB)

God's invisible creative power is at work inside of people. Nothing the designer put inside of us was supposed to stay there. Instead it was designed to flow out of us and benefit the world and the people. God doesn't give us power to do nothing.

Talents, gifts and abilities are power from above to make us greater than ourselves.

With musical power, one can stir the heart and soul with music and singing for pleasure or worship. Others create art or theater that inspires and moves people deeply. Some have the power to be leaders, and to read the hearts of other individuals. With others, their gifts may be the abilities to run like the wind or jump like a gazelle. Yet others create all types of useful inventions. Science and mathematics are gifts. The real object of our storehouse of power is to point to the Greater One or the Gift Giver (God). It is important to acknowledge and honor Him as the source of our power.

It is plain to see that these abilities inside of people are very powerful, because without submitting to God's guidance and purpose, these gifts of ours will produce the self-destructive behaviors of pride, arrogance, greed and emptiness.

Just listen to the headlines about the many celebrities, politicians movers and shakers, and very powerful people who have been made weak through vices, bad habits, bad choices and no real purpose. They only implode and destroy themselves after awhile, because with any power comes the need for great responsibility and accountability.

Responsibility and accountability protect the use of power, as well as the people who are influenced by them.

Ignorance of the Gift Giver and the reason for having these abilities have robbed many from becoming their very best in life. It keeps them operating below the standards they desire for themselves and below the standards of what they were created for.

Take for instance our willpower, our willpower is a gift to us to help protect us. We were designed to use our willpower to keep control over the mind and body from mental and physical breakdown. Sheer willpower has helped some individuals have the courage to go into a burning building to save someone, or it has helped people to lift a car with super human strength.

Your willpower, if you only use it for God. Can help you to boldly choose to get connected to Gods greater good for your life.

When I got connected, that was the day that I began to comprehend the reasons and the whys for things. I was starting to see the invisible at work in my life. Making right choices and right decisions has now become much easier, knowing I will always have God's supernatural help really makes a difference.

Your choices produce success or failure; they open or close doors in your life. Who you decide to be to a great extent, determines the outcome of your future.

So like the Danish proverb states, "What you are is God's Gift to you, what you do with yourself is your gift to God."

Let's consider the power of your voice…

Who is on the other side of your voice?

Who is listening to you or following your advice?

Is it your team, your club or group, or your school, or is it your community? Is it perhaps the world?

Your words carry weight, and you can really affect those who hear you no matter who you are, for good or bad. So you must be determined to speak truth but not lies, peace but not strife, encouragement but not doubt or fear. Use your voice to bring out the best and beauty in others. From the inner treasure of your heart, your mouth will speak.

That is the power of your voice, so if cursing is inside you, it will come out. If hate and violence are in there, they will be voiced.

Your heart is the mirror of the image you reflect.

People are always watching you to see if you are true to your words. And do you do what you say you will?

The invisible inside you can always be seen, one way or another.

Your voice has the power to shape your future and others for good or evil.

But don't use your voice for evil it's a waste of power. It's like bad fruit and tasteless food they will both end up in the trash.

Stop fooling yourself. Garbage in, garbage out.

Get connected to the right source to reflect the right image.

Your Power at Its Best!

Have you ever had feedback about something you did for someone else through your gifts, money or talents that helped changes someone's life for the better?

These changed lives become your greatest rewards down here on the earth, and these rewards are far beyond fame or fortune. When you know that your life has made a difference to someone, it feels heavenly. Believe it or not, that is God's power at work within you; that is how we begin to see the divine side of life at work.

The more we yield and do good for others, the more we affect and change lives for good for the better and for the best.

My all time number-one superhero says in the miracle book, "That I must be about my father's business." The Lord Jesus Christ knew at the tender age of twelve that his power was for the good of us all.

By the age of thirty, His touch opened blind eyes and made the deaf to hear and the lame to walk. He saves the lost.

Your power at its best will give you a life of great rewards and highs. Then you like me, will not want the lowlife of selfishness and evil anymore.

First let God's truth help you uncover lies and fears that control your life so that you will be free to clearly see and operate in love and power. Then you will be able to become the shining light of His goodness.

Chapter 2

THE SOURCE

All of nature around us is fulfilling its purpose except for us humans. The fruit trees the birds and bees, and the sun moon and stars are doing their jobs.

If you plant a seed into the ground and water it, it does exactly what it was designed to do, grow and produce. But who designed the seed to do that?

Inside an idea are the seeds of power towards greatness to accomplish anything. Ideas make way to progress these are God's gifts for all of us.

Visionaries are people who have the power to see what others do not see for the future, about society, culture, business, art, music, technology, and science, and then they can plan for it.

Within nature we can sense this invisible power everywhere. We may not stop to consider its wonderful display or the connection we have to it. Nevertheless, great power is on display every day, wind, rain, lightning, sunlight, DNA etc.

I truly believe that all existence is a miraculous demonstration of supreme power.

So what is a miracle? Most would call a plane crash, where everyone on board walks away from the crash without a scratch, a miracle.

They would say, that such a thing could not have happened without some kind of divine intervention.

What I am exploring in this book is that all life itself is a miraculous divine intervention, and invention. And you will see it if you know how to look at life.

But what is the source? God! That's the quick answer. But how do we humans really grasp or even see things that are invisible to the naked eye? Glad you asked!

In science, we look through special instruments, such as the microscope or telescope to discover things. There have been many important discoveries, that relied on these instruments, and these are discoveries that would have otherwise been invisible.

Case in point, the atoms and electrons, tiny microscopic particles discovered by science. The building blocks of all matter. But how do we see the invisible God and then surrender to Him?

Without sounding too religious, or quoting bible verses, let me say, look at the invisible you, and your hidden wealth of abilities, then you will see God's handy work within you.

Seeing, hearing, smelling, touching and tasting are the doors into the brain, your conscious control tower. Controlling body systems like your digestive system, respiratory system, just to name a few. These are the systems working together to sustain the life of the body.

Biological and chemical information to the brain, your brain is a dazzling celestial universe within.

There are billions of cells in the human body, I call man's earth suit and the body's function is to keep us alive on this planet. For example you can know that a thing is hot or cold because of your sense of touch. The sense of touch tells your brain by shooting electrical signals through your body to avoid the danger of damage. So we experience pain to withdraw our hand.

The five senses also help humankind explore, discover, enjoy and govern the world we live in. **But what is the subconscious mind, or the immaterial you? This is the real you, not the earth suite we live in.**

You can't see thoughts. What is love made of? How can a person touch a person's imagination or joy with their hands? Love and hate are invisible spiritual forces, just as the wind and gravity are invisible natural forces.

Think about it, the God who made the brain to think can teach us and give us divine understanding and revelation as to who He is and who we are to Him.

People can't see everything so our belief system should not be based on seeing is believing.

This type of thinking will only limit you and stop you from experiencing and discovering the Source of Life.

Ancient societies since the beginning of time cultivated belief systems in the invisible, to the point of making up false gods of gold, silver and stone.

Idol worship was in every land and was normal life. The real story of the Source is revealed in the Bible. The true story is that humans are spirit beings just as God is Spirit, with spiritual power working in and through us. Spiritual things may be invisible to the natural eye but they are as real as physical things.

People spend billions of dollars training their bodies, educating their minds, while the real spirit of man is starving and thirsty to be connected back to the Source.

Many in todays society substitute that God hunger for the modern gods of technology, materialism, humanism, sports, entertainment and science.

Worshipping the works of man's hands is the wrong way that is worshipping the creation as opposed to worshipping the Creator. It is because of this foolishness that the mirror of our lives is reflecting the wrong image.

For without submitting to the Master's plan, crime is rampant, broken families are the norm, sickness and disease is common and wars are in every nation.

These things are the evidence that something major is wrong inside of all mankind. Just as fish are designed for water and birds suited for the air and plants use the soil to live healthy. Man as a spirit being must be connected to our Source which is God, to have an abundant good life.

Because some people exert great influence over people's lives, through their prosperity they may be thinking life is great and I don't need an invisible God. But even they will come to realize that their gifts, talents and influence was a blessing from the Greater One for the benefit of us all. Sooner or later…

Many will bask in the light of their own glory and success saying God is only for the weak and poor.

But after a while the emptiness of things without divine purpose will create darkness and vanity. Like a black hole inside of them, sucking any goodness out of them leaving them debased or thinking themselves to be God.

Because the designer of life made His creation to know Him and love Him, these gifts and abilities of ours are little signs to us, saying look up and find the Gift Giver. And the reason for your many blessings.

Once again the emptiness in your life is your God hunger that only He can satisfy.

Some might say, "Hey that's deep! I just want to have fun, have sex, eat, drink and enjoy my life." "What's wrong with that?" My answer is you can it's your choice!

But remember if you give into the craving of your body, you are going down my friend. Once you give into a lifestyle of lust, selfishness and perversion, you lose control of yourself to evil.

The desire to experience pleasure is not bad within itself. The Lord has richly given us all things to enjoy, but not anything He calls evil.

The Creator built us to experience pleasure so that we can understand the pleasure He gets from us, when we love Him and do His will.

Our reasoning and intellect must go beyond the limitation of the five sense realm. Because our senses only limit us to the natural material world.

No one ever saw DNA in past centuries, yet scientists spent years searching inside the human body, seeking that which was invisible, until it became visible.

Someone far greater than DNA is here, God the source of everything. He is invisible yet visible by the things that he has created. Discovering Him will be the difference between you being lost or found or free.

Park your mind on this reality. If you look through the colorful lens of God's love for his creation, you will see God's handy work everywhere.

But if you deny that which is obvious and real, you are playing the fool. Then everything you see will be darkened by that decision.

Seeing the invisible you inside is seeing the invisible Source, to some extent. He made us unique in all His creation, in His image and likeness. (Genesis 1:26) (TLB)

ALL that we taste, touch, see, hear and smell, using our senses is temporary, these bodies will die. But that which is invisible is forever.

We will see life clearer from the sky view, seeing as God sees. It's all in the bestselling book of all time, The Holy Bible. Smart people don't need proof that God exists! The very next breath you take should be proof enough!

Chapter 3

THE TRANSFORMATION

It will take real transformation power for you to become a new you. Your thinking process must change the way you see things. We can observe the development of a little infant that grows from adolescent through teenage years into a young adult. He or she goes through a process of growth and stages to reach complete maturity.

Likewise, animals plants and insects develop in and through stages.

However, in nature there is at least one species of insect that I know of that doesn't grow and develop in stages.

The caterpillar, a worm like insect famous and well known for its developmental process known as a transformation or metamorphosis.

The caterpillar weaves a web like cocoon around itself for a short period of time and then comes out of the cocoon a completely different species known as a butterfly. Now, this butterfly displays its array of stunning metallic colors and flies like a bird with wings.

The word transformation speaks of "a changed form," "a changed appearance," "and a changed inner nature."

The question is, can we as humans experience something like this? Absolutely!!! Let's take a closer look.

We humans are born learn and perceive life by our five senses. Science reinforces this process of development by presenting us with theories and information gained through tests and experiments. People then govern their lives according to what is observed by sense knowledge.

I have come to learn that thinking and reasoning exclusively with our intellect is like limiting ourselves to being like a caterpillar, not a butterfly, when we should be soaring like eagles.

Humans consist and contain much more capacity than what we see with our eyes. Right now all humankind has an opportunity to experience the divine designer's original purpose for us. It is a spiritual transformation to become a brand new creation from the inside out, and to display the beautiful stunning array of God's image and likeness. His divine nature.

This transformation will cause people to go from the ordinary to the extraordinary, from zero to a hero, from the natural to the supernatural, from stressed to blessed, and from the fearful to the powerful.

We all were designed to model God's greatness. Peoples were fashioned to be in God's class of excellence.

But because people's hearts and minds are darkened by evil and sin. The big me, myself and I syndrome. Many are lost and need a savior.

To experience this transformation a new birth must take place first. A birth into the light, a change of heart. If you will, a birth by God's Spirit into His family. That's the good news.

Science has already proven that the universe full of stars and planets began with a "Big Bang" of sorts. That "Big Bang" marked the very moment the Author of Existence spoke those majestic words "Let There Be Light" (Genesis 1) (NKJ). Now you and I must receive that light into our hearts. That is the transformation taking place today.

The clock is ticking, and time is running out on this chaotic evil world. The evidence is obvious, with natural disasters getting grander, and more frequent. And people are getting crazier and more violent than ever.

It would be a crime to withhold important evidence that could save a person's life. If one knew the truth about a court case. This book is that evidence! God's Book is that evidence.

The #1 Image Maker is calling for hate fighters that are full of His love, life savers, healers and lifters, peace makers, those that will be light and act like Him. Yes, and those that will overcome evil by doing good.

It was in the summer of my youth when I chose to believe and receive Christ. So the next time you are outdoors and the sun is shining, look up and feel its warmth and radiance, and then open your heart to the Lord Jesus Christ, God's Love.

Then you too will be transformed and start your journey into His image, from the inside out. The Lord wants to see Himself in you like a mirror.

Chapter 4

THE POWER OF LIGHT

Understanding the Power of Light isn't a religious notion. It is about knowing who we are as people on this planet, and knowing why we exist. It is not to be slaves that is for sure. Slaves aren't free, neither are haters, sex addicts, liars, murders, drug abusers, those that are lovers of pleasure, and all their evil friends.

These people listed above are blind to the truth and cannot see. They are slaves to what they crave and are only living in spiritual darkness. I don't believe anyone of us were born to live like that. So if you want to silence your guilty conscience that screams at you daily, step into the light of change and get help from godly friends.

Which is greater: light that scatters darkness when the light is turned on, or darkness that comes in only because there is absence of light?

The power is in the Light. The power is in the Truth. And in the love of the Truth. We are to let our light shine like a city set on a hill, so that people will see our good works and honor our God.

One of the problems with humankind is that we don't always know what's really going on at times. What's true and what's false. Unfortunately there are so many voices out there. Some have refused to believe in God and good, as they should. Is that you?

Many evils are on the road of life from infant to adulthood. And as a result some may be turned off, and don't care anymore. Then they will wear a sign on their faces saying 'out of order' 'mad as can be,' or 'I am turned off.' The evidence of this is self-centeredness, hatred, unforgivingness, meanness, bitterness, doubt and unbelief, and a hardened heart.

If you are turned off to God and people it means you have no light. It's that simple. To be in the light, a person must love their neighbor as themselves, and honor God. Then change your mind for the mind of Christ.

Take no substitute for the power of truth from the miracle book. The truth will make you free to be the best you were made to be.

You should never resist the light of Christ, for if you hide from his light, you love darkness, if you hide from his truth, then you love lies.

If you hide from love, you love hate. Yes, if you hide from the Lord, you love the devil!

Think about this; your eyes are shaped and designed to receive sun light. In the light we can see clearly and then internalize the sights all around us. But the eyes are useless in the dark. We human beings are fashioned for the light inside and out. We have the finger print of our Maker all over us.

We aren't designed for darkness of any sort. The scripture tells us that God is clothed in unapproachable light. We must desire to be a bright light to a dark world.

Super Insight

How we see life and the way we perceive things will bring out the best or worst in us. For the most part, people tend to look at circumstances through our emotions or our experiences, at times through our will or our influences. Not just our eyes. You may have heard this example, some will see the glass half full, and some people will see the glass half empty. Your views reflect you, your views will frame you like a picture.

If one's heart and mind is darkened, that person will tend to see life in gray, not color. A life filled with doubts, worries, frustrations, fears, no peace, and little or no purpose. The power of this type of person is weakened greatly. It is as if they are trying to see in the dark! The light of faith and truth has to dawn, so that they will be able to realize what they are missing.

Your doubts and unbelief must be told to "get out" boldly. We must invite good things into our lives and look to the future possibilities that God has for us.

The inner eye of perception must be trained. We must practice looking for the good in ourselves and others. Expecting the good, giving out the good, so that the invisible Lord of Good will always show up on our behalf.

Super insight is the power to see without limitations, spiritually and creatively. The highest level of man's creative imagination or inner vision is referred to as genius. A person can be a genius in art, music, military strategies, fashion, to mention but a few.

I believe anyone can be a genius or have a genius moment. If we come to understand it is from God! The designer and Image Maker of life that can and will give any of us the power to excel to accomplish great things. If we will only seek Him for it.

When ideas and concepts flash into our minds, these flashes of inspiration are inspired thoughts from God. Ideas and hunches come through our subconscious mind. These are flashes of inspiration from above, and they will tend to be for the purpose of blessing, helping, encouraging people. Creating good things that will lift humanity if they are from above.

However, most people probably ignore these hunches. Being distracted, dull, too busy or a lack of focus and practice, in capturing these rare gifts.

But make no mistake, these flashes of inspiration are rays of light and power, to be able to see and hear on this level, is from another dimension. Meaning you have the gift to be used, to benefit mankind and yourself.

By reason of use, you will be showing and pointing to the Source. And the Gift Giver, especially if you are humble and thankful to Him. This gives Him all the honor and glory for your super insight.

Since insight is connected to our inner vision and knowledge, the light of insight is extremely important. That is how we begin to see that which is invisible in a visible world.

For instance, who gave all those beautiful flowers all those amazing shapes colors and fragrance, and why? Is it just for bees and pollen perfume and medicines. Or does the Creator simply want us to enjoy the beauty of Himself and His creation.

When people begin to see with the eyes of love and understanding, people places and things appear a lot differently. The world isn't just a wicked sinful place, full of evil and violence. But through God's love, the world is also divinely kissed by a wonderful Maker, who loves us in spite of our many sins and flaws. Now it is because of this great love, my eyes see things through the light of a thankful and grateful heart.

I might be a dreamer but I dream in the day time, and I see life full of possibilities and opportunities for goodness and greatness. Each day I see the sunshine or rain without pay, and I breathe air another day, it's a blessing. When I experience at least one pleasure from LOVE in a special way, it's a gift from above, a gift from LOVE!!!

Love is seeing ourselves through heaven's eyes. Love is walking in the light, not in the dark. We must teach the children this point of view to see that which is invisible, inside of life too.

You may have heard of the Bible story of David and Goliath. David was a young shepherd boy, possibly 16 or 17 years of age, that fought against a giant warrior, at least ten feet tall. David prevailed and killed the giant, for the love of God and his country, but how did David do that?

David's perception and insight of life wasn't ordinary. The way he saw things was extraordinary. David spent most of his time, keeping and tending his father's sheep. To pass the time, David would play his harp and sing praise songs to the Lord his God. David knew God's power was with him because he felt the presence of the Lord as he praised and worshiped Him.

As this true story goes, once a lion and a bear came to snatch a sheep from David's herd, David rose up fearlessly and went after both the lion and the bear and killed them with his sling and stone. Yes power was there with David.

Here is the key; David knew that while he was protecting the sheep, his God was protecting him. David had no fear of Goliath either. The other soldiers in the armies of Israel were very fearful of the giant, and wouldn't go out to battle him. David saw one thing, the fearful soldiers saw doubt and defeat.

The key to having power and to walk in the light is to practice seeing the invisible God of creation. The key also is to learn and do His will. Power is in seeing God's love for us at all times. Just focus on Him by worship and praise for all the good things that He does. Then the Lord will love and protect you also. So arm yourself like David with super insight. Then God will be there with you in the light.

Chapter 5

THE WONDER OF YOUTH

It is wonderful to be young, and to enjoy every minute of it. Taking in every sight and sound, but remember that youth with your whole life before you, one can make some serious mistakes.

So don't let the excitement of being young blind you and cause you to forget your Maker and dishonor Him.

When you decide to honor God in your youth, the Lord will honor and help you throughout your life just like He did for young David, who became the King of Israel.

God Himself will train and teach you to be a champion and winner for Him. So learn all the good you can. The Lord's golden nuggets the Holy Bible are rich with faith love and power, to put you on top.

His blessing and favor will honor and promote you. You will be victorious through every struggle in your life. He gives our lives purpose and meaning that will prepare us for eternity.

When you are young you may have the benefit of time on your side. That is why we must use our time wisely, because it's what you put in the bank of heaven that counts. Remember you cannot take your cars, your clothes or money with you when you leave planet earth.

God's word teaches us how to guard our five senses and guard our affections, from being attacked by evil. The evil of negative thinking, bad attitudes, depression, and the evils of hypocrisy.

So don't vacillate going back and forth between two points of view, faith then doubt. That is being double minded. If you want power from God, you must do what He says in the miracle book. It's just that simple, obey Him.

If you feed your faith, it will grow. If you feed your doubts, your doubts will grow.

Many young believers go to college to have their faith ruined by doubts and unbelief, by not continuing to read their Bibles and praying every day which depletes their faith, making them weak, depressed and eventually losing their way.

They may believe in the Lord alright, but then again try to enjoy everything this world has to offer, even if it is forbidden. The Miracle Book states, "you cannot serve two masters." Remember we conquer evil by doing and being good.

So the question is, are you making God look good or making God look bad?

Sunday morning for many young people that go to church is a big high before the week starts. But by the time Friday and Saturday rolls around, they are either at their lowest low or feeling guilty about every bad thing they let slip in during the week.

Eight keys to staying strong…

1. Let the Lord's heart of love capture your heart to love.
2. What the Lord hates you must never celebrate.
3. God's views must be your good news.
4. Give and receive, receive and give.
5. Stay connected to others in the faith, run from temptations for more transformation grace.
6. Pray about everything, stay in the word and have big dreams.
7. Speak only God's words into your life, and avoid all strife.
8. Stay on guard; repent, not to break the Lord's heart.

The Miracle Book is a unique book unlike any other in the entire world, because it is alive. The Author's power, spirit and love are resident within its pages.

If you want to learn what the designer of life wants from you, it's all in His book, take a look daily.

Rest assured the Lord always watches over His family to bless and help us with miracle power.

Humankind was made to master his world, not to be mastered by the world. The things of this world's system, such as money, celebrity, titles, fortune or fame, should only be tools to use for good. They are not to control you.

People have sold their souls in the pursuit of things until life itself loses meaning, outside the quest for money and stuff.

To love God should be our first, greatest and highest quest in life. Why? Because He made everything you enjoy. So if you want to know what pleases God, that's it? If you don't know Him, pray and ask the Lord Jesus to help you come to know Him.

It bears repeating, God wants all of us to enjoy this wonderful life we have been given. However He wants us to enjoy Him far more with all our heart, mind, soul and strength.

How about taking a minute to thank Him for this day, your health, every breath you take, and for this book that you are reading.

Being a person that is loving and giving towards others is where the power manifests and flows. You cannot give what you do not have. What I am saying in a hundred different ways is get back to the source for a complete image makeover, and a face lift, and to take a look in His book every day, and see if you fit.

We have been given the power and gift of choice. We can choose the taste in foods, the colors we like, the musical sounds, and even the life style we enjoy. So choose to follow what's right, what's good, and what's of Christ light. These are words to the wise.

The Lord is never wicked or unfair. He has all power and authority over the visible and invisible universe, to regulate justice.

"If God were to withdraw His Spirit, all life would disappear, and mankind would turn to dust." (Job 34:14-15) (TLB)

Our Maker is so great, we cannot imagine it and yet He is so just and merciful that He doesn't destroy us for all our evil ways.

According to the Bible, it is written: "The Lord gives power to the weak and to them that have no might He increases strength." (Isaiah 40:29) (KJV)

"Youth shall faint and be weary and fall, but they that wait upon (and serve) the Lord shall renew their strength, they shall mount up with wings like eagles" (Isaiah 40: 30 – 31) (KJV)

This verse says it all. It is time to be an eagle and fly high in all you say and do, while you are still young and alive!

Chapter 6

WHAT IS EVIL?

Webster's dictionary defines evil as devious, deceptive, crafty, wicked, dishonest, and bad natured, corrupt, vicious, harmful, sinful, opposite good and God, pride, arrogance, misfortune, etc. It is the misuse or abuse of something or someone. Evil steals kills and destroys.

So how can you and I be God's champions if we don't know who we are or who our real enemies are?

Everything that exists, whether love, sex, money, religion, music, education, science, toys, sports, can and has been used for good or evil.

Wicked rulers throughout the centuries have oppressed and controlled people using every possible means to their evil ends.

Evil is the void, the emptiness, the darkness or lack of good intentions, or motives. Evil is the enemy of good, it doesn't consider God's will, people's will, justice, fairness, truth, laws, or honesty etc.

Evil seeks to get its own way, evil is seen in constant liars, haters, racism, sexism, envy, jealous, selfish, pride, fear, strife, murder, excessive force, depression, obsession, possession, greed, bitterness, unforgivingness, sexual perverts, lust, mocking, traitor, trouble maker, wild parties, gossip, rebellion, witchcraft, fornication, adultery, idolatry, and all their evil friends.

All of these evils are going to melt away one day. I do believe this worlds' system last hour has come. I am not here to show you how this age will end, but how your new life can begin.

Evil is trying to take down as many people with it as possible. But the good news is this, the light is still shining. Come to the light of Christ, so that you will be forgiven. Supreme love and amazing grace is waiting for you there.

The evils that I have described are some of the attack of spiritual darkness. They may come in the form of temptations, delays, hindrances, deception, or seduction. It is written in the Bible that the whole world is under the sway of the evil one. The real fight and victory over evil is knowing and doing the truth (God's Will). His truth will make and keep you free from the evils tricks and traps. It is all about loving and trusting the Lord only; yes, and having faith in Him.

When God spoke "Let There Be Light", who could stop Him. When He does anything, whoever stops Him? The Lord causes all things to work together for the good of those who love Him in spirit and in truth.

When evil tries to come,

Resist evil (say no! and mean it in Jesus' name.

Learn live and speak God's word – The Bible against evil.

Also, use the Lord's name, but not in vain, because it has power and authority to control all evil spirits.

The Almighty watches everything people and spirits do. God honors those that honor and obey Him.

Don't just complain and cry about all the evils in this world, but get filled with the Holy Spirit of love. And start doing good. "We conquer evil by doing good." (Romans 12:21) (NLT)

You may be thinking, no one cares about me or how I feel. The good news is this, the Lord Jesus cares, and He came to seek and save the lost and hurting. He has all power in heaven and on earth, to help you out of any situation. Just like He helped me.

The one who is getting us dressed and fit for heaven is presenting you and me with miracle keys that are all throughout this book and His Book. Search for them like golden treasures, and priceless pearls. They are here for you.

Just start by thinking about someone else's needs for a change.

Call a neighbor that is hurting, encourage someone, go serve or volunteer, visit someone in the hospital, give away some extra clothes, food or money to one less fortunate. Forgive others crimes against you, and your loved ones too. How about that!

Then good will come back to you. That is a spiritual law. **We reap what we sow**

Just because the whole world is under the sway of evil. Doesn't mean that you and I can't have a little slice of heaven on earth. Right here and right now.

Only try to see The Image Maker's hand at work within you. Shaping and suiting you to be like Him, first class and dressed in excellence. Thank Him when you do.

Chapter 7

POWER TO MAKE A CHANGE

In order to make major changes in one's life, a person must be willing to change their mind-set process. A persons mind-set must be freed from negative stinking thinking. They must stop lying to themselves. And start being honest about their weaknesses.

Ask the Lord in prayer, to help you. He will and desires to change you, from the inside out. That is what the scriptures are all about. And it is impossible for God to lie. (Hebrews 6:18) (KJV)

Why is it impossible, you might ask, and what does that have to do with me changing? Since the Lord is the creator of everything, what He says will be. God creates by speaking, so if God says the sky is red; it would be changed to red to obey His word.

If for instance God spoke to you saying "I have given you a house", it will come to pass if you trust Him and wait for it.

Remember doubt and unbelief are faith's enemies. So starve your doubt and feed your faith by studying and doing God's Word.

Change happens faster when a person refuses to give into their weaknesses, and turn to the Lord for help. This is the meaning of repentance. The Miracle Book says "God is not a man that He should lie." (Numbers 23:19) (KJV)

Let's explore faith a little more, put faith under a microscope. The Good Book says "Without faith it is impossible to please, or perceive God." "For those that come to the Lord, must believe that He exists, and He is a rewarder of them that diligently seek Him. (Hebrews 11:6) (KJV)

Faith comes by hearing God's truth in your heart. Your faith in God brings His invisible power into our visible world, to help and change us into His powerful Image of Light and Love.

Things such as dreams, visions, goals, plans, ideas, and imaginations are part of our fabric that exists on the inside of us. Our faith in God releases his power, to bring these things to pass. You can have faith in yourself, and you can have faith in God. **Faith is the action side of believing. It is not enough to just believe, we must have faith that acts, speaks, and expects results. When you don't have faith in everything, it shows you don't want to do or be anything special.**

God will change and rearrange things in your life, to reflect His Image, when your faith is in Him. Your faith in God produces a transformation in you. "As a man thinks in his heart, so is he." (Proverbs 23: 4) (KJV) What you focus on mentally and spiritually will be drawn to you and will manifest.

Faith in the Lord's goodness, helps us to understand and see things we don't naturally see. God's Word changes us to grasp the reality of the invisible world of God, angels and eternity.

The Bible inspires faith and change, because the Bible is God's holy inspired word. The Bible is His story, His history of dealing with all mankind. The scriptures speak of things beyond our limited world, beyond what is seen with our natural eyes, beyond time and space. Just as DNA was invisible inside the body until discovered.

The change that I am addressing in this book is how God transforms our lives to become the very best they can be. Modeling Christ's likeness and character.

This change will draw divine power to you, it will flow into every fiber of your being. The Lord's joy will over flow through you like a river. Your peace will be sweet like honey less and less stress. God's power and spirit will help you make vital decisions for your life, and for those you help. Divine love in you will conquer all and rise inside you daily like the sun, as you submit and obey Him.

Don't fear these changes, remember no one is perfect, but God. It is all about reflecting the Lord's goodness and letting Him be Himself in you, and through you. **God's favor and grace, will help us reign over the world and serve the people we influence.**

Some may think, because they are well cultured and moral people, that God will welcome them to heaven. These types of people do not try to change, because they feel satisfied with who they are.

But, think about this, you cannot be on a south bound train headed north. No matter how much fun or fast the ride, your destination will never be up north.

Change your train and change your direction, get a one way ticket north, where God lives.

It is not about how good we are, but how good He is, and whether we believe and receive God's gift of eternal life.

"God so loved the world that He gave His only begotten Son, that whosoever believes in Him should not perish but have everlasting life." (John 3:16) (KJV)

"God sent not His Son into the world to condemn the world, but that the world through Him might be saved."
(John 3:17) (KJV)

Yes, I realized what I was missing and where I was going wrong and changed direction.

You have got to stir yourselves to action and compassion; there are billions of people lost and perishing, and you know it. Who is going to be a road block, a stop sign, a hero to rescue them. A witness of God's goodness, it has to be you and I.

We have seen the movies; we all love a happy ending. The Good Book tells us, all that receive the gift of eternal life, win in the end.

One person can change the world and can affect it for good.

Many international organizations that help to rescue millions of people in need have been birthed out of one person's gift and passion.

The Red Cross, Salvation Army, World Vision, Operation Blessings, NAACP, Mothers Against Drunk Drivers, etc. Also businesses and governments have launched programs, because of someone's fight to overcome hunger, poverty, inferiority, or poor services.

These organizations, witness to the power and treasure God has put inside of humanity.

These powerful drives are clues that there are rivers of life flowing from the source of life, giving us a God powered course of action.

Inspirational promptings are powerful, moving people to benefit others. Seek that which flows in you naturally or I might say supernaturally, it is likely from above. His gift of love, power to make a change.

Chapter 8

PRAYER IS POWERFUL

To pray, someone has to first and foremost believe that there is someone out there greater, and powerful enough to answer our prayers and grant our requests.

Secondly, one must realize this fact, the Creator of the universe cares about us, and is always watching and listening.

Prayer is simply talking to the Lord, expecting good to come. Yes, He that has made the ear to hear can hear, and He that has made the eyes to see, can see. Believe it or not, God that has made the mouth to speak can speak.

To have faith for prayer, you must get rid of doubt and unbelief, and simply trust the love of the Lord for us and His creation.

Let's use a little common sense about prayer. If you ask someone for something, you should consider whether or not they have the means to help. And another issue to consider is whether or not they will be willing to help when you ask.

Yes, God says in the miracle book, "I love the world and want to save it."

This brings me to my next point. The Lord of heaven and earth wants us to know Him, His will, and His ways. Then we will truly know how to pray, and what to say.

Finally, once we mature spiritually speaking our prayers will be more about others and less about ourselves.

Prayer is an invitation to become a partner with the living God, and bring His will and good into this evil world.

When you see something bad on the web, TV, or the news, don't just talk and complain about it, but pray and be a part of the solution.

You can see the reality of the Creator in the things He has made. If you look, you will see. The designer wants people to recognize His power and influence, not just the evil ones influence.

When we notice a shining new BMW cruise down the street, the workmanship and excellence that went into the car's superior design is obvious. No doubt this is an expensive car.

So how is it we can gaze at this vast universe, including ourselves, and then dismiss the existence of a Supreme Being? To me, to deny Him is to be blind and dumb in your mind.

It's very foolish to say, I don't believe or pray because I don't believe in what I don't see. Things we cannot see sustain our very existence

- The air we breathe
- Energy
- Thoughts
- Love
- Belief itself
- Gravity etc.

The unseen is seen if you will look! The Supreme Being says in the Bible, "The earth is the Lord's and everything in it belongs to Him." (Psalms 24:1) (KJV)

The Lord is not out of order, its humankind who is out of order. Our prayers and faith draws Him close to us. Compared to the Lord, the whole earth is but a drop in the ocean.

So why does God the Almighty even bother with us? Because he loves us. He said that he made us to be like Himself, and He is the Image Maker.

The Most High and Most Beautiful One is sending an invitation for all to come and talk with Him. Yes, come he says "let's reason together, and gets rest and peace for your souls." (Isaiah 1:18) (KJV)

So, let His peace be the empire of your mind, calling the shots. God's peace should be the atmosphere around your every decision. For in that state of peace, your mind will be fully charged, like a powerful generator.

Prayer and God's presence brings times of refreshing, moments of inspiration and power. Why? Because you can only give to others what you have. People cannot give what they do not have!!!

The Lord doesn't want us to worry or be fearful about anything, yet we humans worry and are fearful about every little thing. Yes, we are out of order and only our Maker and Savior can help us and fix our brokenness and image.

We humans are of great value to our designer. That is why, His call and invitation is to all people everywhere to come to Him.

Give the Lord's air back to Him in prayer. Talk to Him daily about your problems, He fixes what is broken when we ask Him to. Take a break and pause from the mess of this world and breathe the fresh air of prayer. He will hear you, if you will only believe in Him.

Do this first, honor God and reverence Him as the great Giver and Father He is. Be thankful, forgive others, pray for others, and ask to be forgiven in Christ's name.

The Lord delights in peoples' prayers, sincere prayers, honest prayers, humble prayers. Your prayers show God you really believe in Him and in His love.

For with God all things are possible.

Prayer power isn't for us to show how spiritual we are, but to see God's will being done on earth as it is in heaven (AMEN).

Chapter 9

THE POWER OF JOY

Is there a real difference between joy and happiness? Or are they both mere emotions that overflow from within us when things are well?

A person generally lives in a state of happiness as life circumstances work out for them. So then sadness would be the opposite of happiness. As things go wrong, circumstances would produce disappointments discouragements, leading to sadness.

The emotion of sadness and happiness are stimulated by outside stimulus. However, joy doesn't operate that same way.

Joy is an invisible force that is generated by our willpower and it expresses itself from the inside outward. Joy also is a gift from God, that you can ask for and receive. God's kingdom is love, joy and peace in the Holy Spirit that will come and live inside of your heart.

Then, you can live in a state and atmosphere of joy, no matter what is happening in your life. Joy will be your strength.

Joy flows from the heart and can shield you against the evil forces of worry, sorrow, depression, and fear. To rejoice in the Lord sustains and preserves those that do it.

To have the joy of trusting in the Lord Jesus is to have the power to walk on the waters of troubles in your life. Joy is expressed by a giving heart, a willingness to love whether you are up or down.

Joy is the medication for your soul; it produces the right attitude, and a humble grateful heart in the face of crisis or suffering.

We all were tailor made for joy, because when a person becomes sad and gloomy, it starts to work against their health and they seem to color everything they experience with negativity and darkness.

Even science has observed with people that are joyful, that the brain becomes more active. Joyful people are open to be friendly. Joyful people are more lighthearted and lively.

Joy is a spiritual force that will illuminate you, like a spotlight, you will be noticed. Real joy warms hearts and making others feel better.

Joy stops strife and contention in its tracks. The fruit of joy is packed with tasty flavors that many can enjoy.

To keep your joy red hot, look for the good in every situation and circumstance. Look to the promise of the Lord that everything works together for the good of those that love God and are called to His purpose.

Guard your joy, and joy will guard you.

Chapter 10

THE POWER OF PURITY

In every chapter of this book, I am trying to connect the reader with the indescribable and extraordinary virtues and gifts that are necessary to become the great and the powerful in God's image. To help you successfully take off the poor garments of darkness, fleshy cravings, and insecurities.

This one virtue is a must have, and is at the top of my list, for the makeup of your life.

God is Holy and cannot be compared to anyone or anything else in the universe. Purity and holiness through Christ helps us to see Him without eyes.

The power of purity forms inside of those that embrace the Lord and His values with a sincere heart. Embracing His virtues and values to work in and through their lives. As a result of purity, your heart will become more and more untainted, uncontaminated by the evils of this world. Having just a child like openness towards this gift of life.

However, it all starts with believing and receiving God's Son Jesus Christ for the forgiveness of sin that God freely offers to every one without condition.

Why is it so important to have such purity operating within us? The Bible states that "Blessed are the pure in heart, for they shall see God." (Matthews 5:8) (KJV) To see God is to become more like Him.

A person who is pure in heart looks for and sees the good in things. "But a person who is negative and untrusting finds evil in everything, for a dirty mind and rebellious heart colors all they see and hear." (Titus 1:15) (TLB)

To make something pure, such as gold, it has to be put through fire, or some type of process that will get the impurities out. When the heart of man is examined by God, his or her deepest motives, desires and intentions have to be purified. God tests and proves the heart of man. Purity is what the Lord desires from each of us. He gives us a choice to choose between good over evil, clean over dirty, right over wrong, light over darkness, blessings over curses, life over death, holy over unholy.

If you choose correctly, then you will be given just rewards from the Lord. Your obedience and willingness to be in His image and likeness will bring the armies of heaven to your defense.

This journey of life is the Lords' purifying process for those that choose Him.

Because people can choose what they like and dislike, everybody will be held responsible and accountable to the Image Maker for their choice. All manner of unclean and ungodly desires arise when someone loves and chooses evil, sin and darkness instead of good and light. But, oh the joys of those who purify themselves and delight in being made beautiful by the Lord.

A good tree is known by its good fruit, and an unhealthy tree's fruit is good for nothing. No matter what a person might look like or their words say, their actions will define them. Purity is a powerful force that brings God's presence case in point. Who has walked this earth in history more pure and powerful than Jesus Christ? A healer, miracle worker, lover of people, the Savior, and the perfect model of God's life style.

Who will ascend to heaven? (The Psalmist David asked) "But those with clean hands, and a pure heart." (Psalm 24:3-4) (KJV) **The word of God is very pure, cleansing the heart and renewing the mind. It will transform a person into a soldier of love, lover of truth, a warrior of light.**

Even the wisdom we can receive from above is pure and peaceful, helping to purify our ways. So that others will see the light of God in and through our good deeds.

There are many religions around the world that believe in the afterlife, and speak of going to paradise, and that's good. I hope we all make it.

But remember it is written, that only the pure in heart will see God. So start today, get rid of all the dirty unclean things out of your life, things that you know are wrong for you. The things that don't please God, that are against His will. Then you will truly have a heart of gold and people will see the Lord in you!

Chapter 11

PEACE MAKER

Peace = quiet, rest, stillness, contentment, harmony, ease, tranquility to your soul.

The way you perceive life can make your life seem like a storm of conflicts and commotions, or a sea of peace. It all depends on your point of view. There are constant conflicts, wars and battles of the mind, between body and spirit, rich and poor, males and females, young and old, and other cultural dysfunctions. These conflicts can be a daily source of irritation to those that are engaged in them.

People have raging wars within them, that are fueled and influenced by abuses, bad habits, a weak mind, no willpower, also no spirituality. These influences can be at the core of a person's lack of peace.

It is written in the Word of God that, "If people would keep their minds fixed on the Lord, then He will keep them in perfect peace." (Isaiah 26:3) (KJV) A peace that surpasses all understanding. How? By studying the scriptures, and living by its power.

Beyond all that we see and don't see, we must know this; God cares about us so we shouldn't worry or fear. The Lord has the power to help us through every bad situation that may come our way.

There is peace in trusting in the Lord and in His Word, and not in our own limited understanding of things. We humans are wired to enjoy the beauty of a sunset, the serenity of a park, a beach or a lovely garden. People love flowers, rainbows, waterfalls, forest and mountains.

However, many don't stop to enjoy them or gaze up at the stars, being too caught up in the rat race, if you will. The noise and busyness of city living can really stress a person out. Almost forcing them to find a quiet place, or peaceful moment.

Finding simple pleasures is what our Maker wants us to enjoy. Christ says, "Blessed are the Peacemakers, for they shall be called the children of God." (Matthews 5:9) (KJV)

How do we become peacemakers when we don't have any peace to give, and don't know how to make it?

The Lord's image and likeness includes the power of peace. He wants you and I to get peace from Him. He is our peace, and then we can take and make peace wherever we go.

Giving peace to others in need is like giving water to the thirsty. To be set free from daily worries and stresses of life is a great gift.

The Lord Jesus says, "Live one day at a time and God will take care of your tomorrow's." (Matthews 6:34) (TLB) This is the way of life to those that trust in the Lord.

Always seek the Lord's help for your life because that pleases Him. Think about it, if you can't do anything about your problems from time to time. Then, why worry... Know without a doubt that all people young and old are extremely valuable to God. The proof is Christ's death on the cross for our sin.

A King, Queen President or Prime Minister's word is backed by great power. How much more the Word of God, who created everything, whether visible or invisible. Since the creator keeps the universe and the world from falling apart completely, surely He can and will help you to be at peace!

If you have been seeking peace through sex, drugs or any other addiction or religion, it is time for you to invite the Prince of Peace to come and live inside of you.

Ask Christ for forgiveness, He will give this wonderful gift to you. It's His promise. Then you too will experience the gentle stream of peace flowing inside you, with waves of love.

The Lord has made peace with all mankind, so fear not, and only believe. Then He will make you His ambassador of peace. "But there is no peace to the wicked, says the Lord." (Isaiah 48:22) (KJV)

Chapter 12

THE GREATEST GIFT GIVER

God so loved the world that He gave!

Think about it. What can you give the one who has everything. The earth belongs to God! Everything in all the world is His!

The two greatest gifts that God has given to all mankind are:

- The gift of life, for without life we don't exist to enjoy or experience anything.
- Eternal life, for with this gift you get to go to heaven, not to hell, after our short life span here on this planet.

However, this second gift must be asked for and received through God's beloved Son, Jesus Christ.

Gifts always come from somewhere or someone. What man or woman gave the brain its thinking ability, or awareness and consciousness? These are gifts from God. Who but God gave the multi functioning systems of the body working together as one unit? That is why the Lord is the Greatest Gift Giver.

Scientific studies says that a bee should not be able to fly because of the size of the bee's little wings, compared to the size of its body. But the bee does fly very well, and that's its gift.

An eagle flies high and lives in the cliffs of mountains and tall trees. So guess what? An eagle's eye sight is four times sharper than a man with perfect eye sight. The eagle can fly as high as ten to twenty thousand feet in the sky. That ability to see for miles is a gift from God.

Gifts and the power that is given to humanity are to ensure our success and ruler ship over the earth. Remember earth is only the beginning of man's journey.

You must receive the gift of eternal life to have an everlasting future.

One of the main attributes that has marked several great citizens in history, is their willingness to give of themselves to help others, and to be dedicated to see others benefit from their sacrifices. They are noted for bringing people together for a greater good, or inspiring others to reach higher heights in life. To name a few, Winston Churchill, Mother Teresa, Martin Luther King Jr, Abraham Lincoln, Cesar Chavez, Gandhi, Billy Graham etc.

As we have freely received, we are to freely give, no matter what, love, money, joy, peace, courage, or a helping hand. Name it and give it.

But if you are selfish and are fearfully holding back when it comes to giving to others. That selfishness and fear is not God's will for you. For the Lord gives sunshine and rain to the just and unjust, to the good and the evil. "If you love only those who love you, what good is that? For even evil people do that." (Matthews 5:45-46) (TLB) You are not imitating God acting like that.

When you love and give to the unthankful and unlovely then and only then, are you reflecting God's image and likeness. You show by acts of love that you are serving the Living God and pleasing Him. Remember, when you give it will be given back to you, and God will honor and reward you for it.

What our wonderful Maker wants all of us to learn and model is that living is giving and giving is a living seed, we plant for more good to grow. We should be producing a healthy character in our lives for others to see.

Giving is a spiritual power that battles greed and selfishness, cheating, envy, jealousy, and all their evil friends. Being a greedy stingy person stops blessings from flowing and reaching the people who need them the most. If you are selfish like I've described you can have so much more, if you only give more.

So don't hold on too tight to anything but the Gift Giver Himself. There is power in your gifts, talents and abilities too, as Michael Jackson sang "Make this world a better place, for you and for me and the entire human race."

"God loves a cheerful giver." (2 Corinthians 9: 6-7) (KJV) Why? Because God Himself is a cheerful giver.

This verse is a supreme revelation about the character of God. Great favor and blessings will come to cheerful givers.

The Lord wants all of us to hit the target of our destiny by aiming for love and a giving lifestyle. That is how we were built.

All of our goals, dreams and ambitions should flow out of a desire to be a blessing to others, and please the Lord who has gifted and blessed us.

When we offer ourselves and who we are back to the Lord from our hearts, then God will use and favor us to bless the world we influence and impact.

Remember according to Genesis, the original plan for man in the Garden of Eden was to enjoy everything, good and very good for free. Fast forward, thousands of years since Adam and Eve our first parents, it is written, "No eye has seen nor ear has heard what God has prepared for those who love Him." (1 Corinthians 2:9-10) (KJV) This is a future event, earth is only the beginning of man's journey.

So listen closely, if you don't believe and receive the Lord's message, how will you get what He has prepared for you? Even more important, how can you be used for His glory if you don't believe Him?

What I am saying in this book is that lots of people everywhere, are fully enjoying God's gifts, life and blessings, but don't give God a second of their time. If you were to put a microphone in people's faces and asked them, "How often do you pray, or spend time reading the Bible?" Many would say almost never.

The Gift Giver sustains all the earth and feeds men and beasts on it. The Lord holds the entire universe together, giving us fruitful seasons, breath, sunshine, rain, but people act as though man is in control. But with a little disaster, we feel hopeless without God's help.

But to you, that are wise reading this book! Your love for God is that missing ingredient in today's society. He makes it all work better but without Him there is trouble. I believe the Lord is giving all people everywhere a chance to choose Him. The Lord has said again and again "You cannot love God who you don't see without loving those that you do see." In closing, meditate on this, **"Heaven would feel like hell to an evil, selfish wicked person who doesn't love God or obey Him, first on earth."**

But heaven will be a paradise of bliss to a cheerful giver, who gets to know God's love down here on earth.

The Great Gift Giver is giving all a personal invitation to give back to Him, forever.

Chapter 13

LOVE POWER

If I were to ask people what is love; I would more than likely get a myriad of answers as diverse as people's imaginations. They would probably reduce love to having very strong feelings and emotions toward someone or something. Perhaps, be it love for a car, love for a dog, and or love for a country.

But, love is so far beyond mere feelings, attractions and emotions. I say this often referring to love. "Love is like the sun in full strength, shinning down on all of us, giving life to everything." "Love is like the air we breathe, its invisible." But everyone would know when air or love is not present. To me love is the essence, the rhyme, and the reason for all existence.

Why would anything exist if not for a reason, or for a purpose. And sense things have a purpose, who gave it its purpose?

The reason why is the clue, it is for the Maker's pleasure that things were created, for the Maker's Love.

Think about it, if you made an apple pie, the pie would exist to be eaten by you or someone else, or just to be looked at, that is also a reason.

In the Holy Bible (Genesis 1&2), it is written "Everything the Lord made was good and very good." That was the Image Maker's desire for everything.

The only thing that was forbidden was the fruit of the tree of knowledge of good and evil. The Supreme Being was giving mankind choice. He said they could eat freely from every tree but, "If you eat from the forbidden tree, you will surely die!" **Good and evil mixed together is deception, don't eat the fruit of deception it will kill, steal and destroy you.**

They were warned about the tree and its fruit. Love will always warn us. **Choosing to obey is fruit that you love God.**

If Adam and Eve had listened to love's warning, no harm would have come to them or us.

The Lord of love declares His purpose for things in the first book of the Holy Bible, study it!

Love is packed with power and purpose, love is invisible, but can be seen, felt, and displayed in many ways.

A person can't just think love, it is too powerful for mere thoughts, love has to come to the light, and it has to be visible if it is real love; by specific actions and deeds.

Love needs expression, demonstration. Love is God's greatest commandment, love is the only true sign that God is in people's lives.

Love conquers hate and evil with good deeds. Love brings people back to life from dead ways, listen to this true story.

A friend told me about a husband and wife from New York who shared this story at a church service. The woman's husband treated her pretty bad for years, he would do things like this:

On the weekends and sometimes during the week, her husband would come home very late after midnight, very intoxicated with friends demanding that his wife get up and fix food for them.

The husband's friends would often object, but her husband would insist. She would get up each and every time and serve them.

The wife never complained or argued with her husband in front of his guests.

One day the husband asked her, "Why do you just get up without fighting with me?" (Now everybody take note of her answer)

She answered, "When I die I know where I'm going, I'm going to heaven and when you die I know where you are going, you are going to hell. So I am trying to make life better for you before you go there." Wow!

The next Sunday, the husband got up with his wife and went to church and gave his life to the Lord and has never been the same.

That is the real power of love, in action, a changed life.

The wife overcame many evils with the right understanding and by not fighting with her husband; she was both saving herself and him from heartache and stress.

Walking in love is where the power shows up.

Powerful unconditional love was put on display; she became her husband's superhero. They both were transformed into God's image of love.

People use those three words (I love you) so casually, that love has almost lost its meaning.

Love is not an impulse or rush of emotions or zing of lustful attraction. Because all of these types of emotions are temporal and cannot sustain real love, against the storms and earthquakes of life.

Truelove is a gift, a special gift that brings people together and then makes them greater than themselves, as they make a commitment to be a blessing to each other. Unselfishly, unconditionally, shining as one person.

People have to surrender to love to experience love's power in their lives. Perfect love has no fear and will cause you to hate strife, selfishness, arrogance, pride, bitterness and un-forgiveness.

A transformation takes place within a person's heart, when love is king. That's the place where a person can think about pleasing others more than just pleasing themselves. Such as going the extra mile for someone when you don't feel like it. And loving your enemies because you can see just how lost they really are. With God's love inside you, you will be able to pray blessing and favor over those that treat you unfairly. The key here, is once you have received the Lord's unconditional love into your life, then you can freely give the gift you have received.

God is the 1st to love, because everything you say you love, He made it.

Since the greatest commandment is to love God and love people, then the greatest sin is not to love God and not to love people. When you do everything with love, then love will touch everything you do!

When we are clothed and dressed with our Maker's likeness, we can look for opportunities to be the love just like him. Giving support, comfort, rescuing the hurting, helping and uplifting, and also inspiring people just like Him. Not because of what you can get from doing good, but what you can bring to the situation. The Miracle Book states that, "If I do not have active love (charity), I am nothing." (1 Corinthians 13:2) (KJV)

The stamp of approval is to love unconditionally, certain people take pride in only love for their close friends, family, country, culture, etc. But aren't open to others outside their group, clicks, status, ethnicity or crowd. This is a portray of conditional love and not God's best and will only lead to hate, pride, division, envy, jealousy, racism, just to name a few. That is wearing the rags of a poor self image hence making you unfit for the Master's use. I ask people like that, "Who's your daddy, God or the devil?"

"Love is very patient; love is kind, never jealous or envious, never boastful or proud or selfish or rude."

"Love doesn't hold grudges and will hardly even notice when others do it wrong."

"It is never glad about injustice but rejoices with truth. If you love someone, you will be loyal to them no matter what the cost."

"You will always expect the best of them and always stand your ground in defending them." (1 Corinthians 13:4) (TLB)

This is a picture and the image of love's character and is God's best for us. We must yield to it and strive to do it. "Special gifts from God will someday come to an end, but love goes on forever." (1 Corinthians 13:8) (TLB)

Let's make up our minds right now, that unconditional love will be our greatest goal, our greatest quest. To be love conscious at all times instead of self conscious.

The Lord has placed mankind over the works of His hands. In order to rule over the earth and the beast, God has given us power that should be obvious, by man's advancement.

Since love is the greatest power of all in the universe, then why don't we see more of it on display in the world?

We do see sex, its everywhere, TV, movies, magazines, music, and the internet. So, is sex love? Sex may be an expression of love but love is much deeper and far reaching than the thrill of sex.

It is a mistake to confuse sex with love. Refuse to be ruled by your body.

There are four types of love we experience:

1. Physical love: (Greek) Eros, erotic love between couples hopefully in marriage.
2. Family love: (Storage) love between parents and children.
3. Love of choice: (Agape) unconditional, unselfish giving love without fear, worship love for God.
4. Brotherly love: (Phyla) strong friendship, royalty, respect, support.

Agape, is the love we humans are designed to display, exude and model. The love that can change a no good husband or bitter wife. Agape love transforms nations and people from the inside out.

This love is supernatural and powerful, it covers other's weakness, and it helps you to obey God's will.

Unconditional love will resist evil, and make it flee. It is the evidence that God lives in you and you walk with Him.

Before creation ever came into being, before matter, energy, light, earth and man, there was love!

As for me, the highest and greatest revelation in the entire universe is; GOD is love! GOD is love! GOD is love! (1 John 4:8) (TLB)

What are human made of? I say 100% love, 100% spirit. It is love's power that created the heart of man, if you believe.

Heaven is where God's presence lives and He wants us to experiment His presence, and carry it to the lost here on earth.

The designer fashioned us to be in His image and likeness, because He loves us all. God built a paradise for Adam and Eve, in the Garden of Eden. He put out first parents there to be His children of love to fill the earth with love and make earth our paradise.

But evil came in and stole their hearts with lies and deception, away from the Lord.

The Bible is God's story of how He spent thousands of years getting his family back in love with Him.

Because Adam and Eve were warned, but still willingly gave up their control to evil. All mankind has to come back to the Lord willingly.

God's supreme love was demonstrated once and for all in the life, death and resurrection of His Son Jesus Christ, a ransom and substitute for our disobedience and rebellion against God's love.

Christ paid the price on the cross; now God's arms are wide open, inviting all to come! If that story sounds too good to be true, it's not! It is real, and it is for you now!

The Bible is His History, how man was made like God not a fallen angel, Satan.

God's wonderful love is so powerful and forgiving, that He would not let us go. He is full of compassion and Amazing Grace.

Yes, history has witnessed the greatest love story ever told and the world will never be the same again.

LOVE IS IN CONTROL!

Chapter 14

POWER TO EAT - POWER TO CHOOSE

A sensible person eats to live while a greedy person lives to eat, and never gets enough.

The profit of the earth is for all, and all the labor of man is for his mouth, and his appetite drives him along. But if you are feasting on unhealthy or harmful things, they will cause you to become sick. This sickness may happen to your body, mind or spirit, if you are out of control.

Because people can choose what they like or dislike, we have the power to take the good and reject the bad. That is why you are ultimately responsible; you alone guides food into your mouth or let sights and sounds into your mind.

Companies try to sell people just about everything, but the power to consume or buy it is purely in your control.

In the future, take note of the kinds of appetites you enjoy or the kind of things you allow in your life, be it, people, places or things. **As you may have observed in all nature, everything produces after its own kind. That is divine order, apple seeds make apple trees, chickens do not make fish and fish do not produce cows.**

This process of reproduction operates both in the visible and invisible worlds.

It functions in the spiritual, mental and physical realms. Negative thoughts will produce more negativity; poor food chooses produce poor health. Hate and evil can be seeds planted in your life that will grow like weeds if not uprooted.

Our first parents (Adam and Eve) chose to eat the forbidden fruit that produced sin and death.

My question to you is, what forbidden fruit are you eating or consuming today? What forbidden lifestyle have you adopted, because of popular culture? Because of your choices, you may end up eating the bitter fruit of having your own ways.

You and I make choose the good over evil no matter how appealing evil appears to be. I have come to see that is what the school of planet earth is all about, choosing the good!

No matter how weak or how desperate or how hungry, people do not go to the toilet to find something to eat, excuse me for being so raw!

The reason being we don't go there, is because there is only waste there.

So why are we letting our minds and bodies be filled with so much waste or junk foods, drugs, bad movies, music, books, etc, in the name of pleasure and entertainment? Why are we so out of order?

Use your will power, or the Lord's power, but resist the unhealthy and forbidden fruit of an evil world. A world that is drunk on its own freedom of choice.

Power has to flow to be active, resist temptation, resist consuming all the evil that is being marketed and pushed on us every day. Be it porn, gluttony, racial superiority, greed, lust, sexual perversion in any form, is nothing but a waste, seeds of evil sin and death. It is extremely necessary to understand not only the natural world, but also the spiritual world of the Bible, because it is real. We must bear the image of the godly and not just the earthly. We can be filled with living energy, light, joy, peace, and love like Christ.

Red, yellow, black and white is not the LIGHT! Do not give up your power or other forces will use your power to control you. Evil will play you like a violin.

Take control of what you consume it is your birth right as human beings on this planet to be healthy, spirit soul mind and body. If people were not so valuable then so many forces would not be trying to take control of us. Stealing our identity with God and using us as their consumers, slaves, followers, selling us the wrong image of the wrong spirit.

One rotten apple can spoil a whole barrel of apples. This illustration is not referring to uneatable fruit, but rotten people who spoil a lot of good people. If you do not remove the bad apples from your life, then they will only make you sick like them.

It's your choice to show the beautiful light and character of the Image Maker. You must choose Him and reflect Him. Lets put on the beautiful garments of His righteousness. How do I do that it seems so hard you might ask?

Keep your focus on who He is in you and through you! The Maker of all that is good, pure and godly.

Taste and see that the Lord is good!

The Bible says, "God has given us richly all things to enjoy." (1 Timothy 6:17) (KJV) But not forbidden things.

So eat and drink in the moments that fill your life with love joy peace and laughter.

You have been given by God the power to choose, because we are wonderfully made to be like Him. So, feast on the rich and good fruit of God's love for mankind. Then the forbidden fruit of evil becomes less and less appealing.

The tree of the knowledge of good and evil has fruit that is full of lies deception and death.

Whether seen or unseen evils, leave them far behind for your own good, and get hungry for the truth!

Chapter 15

WISDOM AND COMMON SENSE

The book of Proverbs states, "Wisdom cries in the streets." This is a spiritual metaphor of how the spirit of wisdom is eagerly reaching out to help, all mankind excel in life. But how are we to know for sure it is the voice of wisdom from above that is speaking? Wisdom's voice directs people to reverence the Lord.

Wisdom's voice, gives common sense, good advice, discernment, insight, integrity, fairness, honesty, discretion, purity, and sound judgment. A life that is filled with foolishness, selfishness, vanity, fear, worry, cruelty, pride, naivety and negativity is just the opposite of wisdom.

In the Holy Bible, wisdom is the main thing, Proverb states, "Getting wisdom is the most important thing you can do!" (Proverbs 4:7) (TLB) The ability to see clear with understanding and comprehend that which is hidden behind someone's action or words is a gift.

Wisdom is also, knowing the difference between right and wrong.

You don't get wisdom just because you're a member of the human race, if that was the case, more people would be operating out of a wise and not foolish mind.

Wisdom is such a precious gift from God, that God himself puts his stamp of approval on those that have it.

King Solomon, a king of Israel was such a person; Solomon was considered the world's wisest man in his time.

Chapter 16

WISDOM

So how did he get such wisdom that made his name renowned through the ages? Solomon simply asked God for wisdom, with all his heart and he promised the Lord he was willing to use it to benefit others.

The Lord used Solomon to write three of the books of the Holy Scriptures, and one is a must read to gain wisdom called Proverbs.

I called the book of Proverbs, "A dance with wisdom." Have that dance daily as a part of your divine image makeover. Wisdom can and should be applied to just about any and every situation in your life.

Chapter 8 of Proverbs states, "The voice of wisdom calls all to love good and hate evil." The reverent fear of God is the beginning of wisdom. If a person doesn't respect or consider the Lord's will as part of their lives, how can they possibly have wisdom, God's precious gift flowing through them?

Before anything was created in the visible world, wisdom had to be there in existence with God, because it took divine wisdom to create the world with all its complexity and order.

Before the earth and all its marvels, yes, wisdom was the craftsman at the Lord's side. When the designer made the blueprint for all creation and its splendor, wisdom was there at work.

Now, young and old should listen and follow after wisdom's instructions and wise counsel. For whoever gets wisdom, also wins the Lord's favor.

"By wisdom's strength kings reign in power, and do rule." (Proverbs 8:15) (TLB) Wisdom also says, "I love all who love me and those that search for me will find me and get unending riches, honor and righteousness." (Proverbs 8:17-18) (TLB)

"To find and get wisdom is life, but to refuse wisdom is to love death." (Proverbs 8:35-36) (TLB)

An awesome force to defeat and overcome evil in your life is the power of wisdom. So do not leave home without it!

When I speak of wisdom, I am aware that there are two distant types of wisdom. There is an earthly or worldly wisdom that is based on craftiness inspired by pride, greed, lies, deception and lust for power.

Many notorious criminals, world leaders, business and political masterminds have used their lust for riches to rule and conquer many. Godly wisdom hates pride, arrogance, deceit and corruption of every kind.

Uncontrolled ambition has motivated many people to become schemers in their pursuit of wealth and power but using worldly wisdom does not lead upward on the high road of integrity and fairness, but downward on the low road of corruption and destruction.

These types of people usually have no regard for the consequences of their actions, and leave behind a trail of devastation.

But the wisdom that comes from God above is first of all, pure, humble, gentle, easy going, courteous, and willing to yield to others.

Divine wisdom is full of mercy and goodness, noble, sincere, good willed, straight forward and inspired to make peace. No evil or darkness is in it. Read the Bible's book of James chapter 3 starting at verse 13, to get a better understanding.

Divine wisdom promotes and protects those that have it. There are many beautiful pictures and benefits painted by wisdom for us in the miracle book of Proverbs, Psalms and Ecclesiastes. **Take a look and see if you fit.**

Our designer's wise instructions are His riches to be discovered. A person's heart must diligently seek and search for them. Ones soul must ask and cry out to the giving Lord for His wisdom. Then listen daily and look for godly wisdom to speak and show up...

When I started to obey God's will, He gave me more and more understanding and insight into Himself and what is the point of existence. And what on earth are we here for.

People are pursuing riches, fame and fortune with total abandonment, but, how much more should they be pursuing God and wisdom which are far greater and more valuable than fame and fortune. Because wisdom comes from God's own mouth and can bring about riches, goodness and peace of mind.

When wisdom comes into your heart, it is like sweet honey to your soul. Wisdom takes away the darkness, the fog and the confusion in your life.

Information comes from many sources, but wisdom comes from the Lord himself. The Lord's favor comes to the humble not the proud. The Lord wants our trust and confidence to be in Him and not in ourselves, and our own abilities.

Remember to be a wise, faithful, healthy person. One must stay connected, at all times, to the source, God, and his values.

Wisdom comes to those that have a hunger and thirst for it. To those that eagerly desire to know the Lord and model his ways.

When you desire to welcome truth and wisdom into your life, then and only then, will you leave behind your foolishness, naivety and negative ways. You cannot keep hanging around fools and be wise. You cannot keep saying NO to God and His ways, and expect Him to say YES to you.

The Bible says, "One wise person will know how to deliver a city from an army camped against it." (Ecclesiastes 9:15) (TLB)

"Being wise is as good as being rich. In fact, it is better because you can get anything by either wisdom or money." (Ecclesiastes 7:11-12) (TLB)

"A wise person is stronger than the mayors of ten big cities." (Ecclesiastes 7:19) (TLB)

How to apply wisdom to everyday life is called common sense.

Chapter 17

COMMON SENSE

First thing I must say is that common sense is not common.

Common sense is wisdom applied practically through our thinking, sensible, rational and reasonable. Also, it is the ability to apply facts to the circumstance of your life for the best possible outcome.

<u>Three examples of common sense:</u>

1. The company you work for is having financial problems and employees are being laid off. But you decide to ask your boss for a raise in salary. Even if you deserve a raise, your timing lacks common sense and you will probably get fired for asking.
2. You really like that special someone, you get their phone number and keep calling and texting them but he or she is slow to return your calls. NEWS FLASH!!! Their just not into you, so move on. That's common sense.
3. You've been hanging around friends you like, but they seem to have fun making you the object of their jokes, calling you silly names etc. You have been trying to get them to stop and you respectfully overlook their insults, but they refuse to stop. They aren't really your friends and may even be jealous of you, or just bad people. Find new friends or get used to those silly names. That's common sense.

Common sense is having good judgment, simply knowing how and when to act. It also knows what to do or say in challenging situations. Common sense is the ability to be smart in everything you do, and are facing.

Only fools do not want to be taught and fools lack common sense. Fools are people who fight the facts, then miss the target their aiming at.

Without common sense and wisdom a person cannot distinguish between right and wrong, good or evil. Common sense gives power to stay away from harm and evil.

The Lord does not want any of us to be troubled. He doesn't want our world to be out of order with things constantly going wrong.

However, to prevent a world full of trouble, God supplies wisdom and common sense. But these gifts have to be received and applied. If you desire favor with God and man, you need these heavenly gifts in your life. Do not trust in yourself alone because you could deceive yourself. Common sense will direct you and crown your efforts with good success. Wisdom will be the craftsman by your side, your guide and captain of your ship.

If you do not have wisdom and common sense, how can you give good advice or excellent counsel to others?

Without wise leadership, for example, a nation is in trouble. Safety comes in a multitude of counselors; wisdom helps people see a life of beautiful possibilities, where foolishness limits people and puts them in the dark. To avoid the pit falls on the road of life, get all the wisdom and common sense you can to see what is ahead. A fool does not see and will even brag about it. Thinking they know it all.

A wise person eyes are in their heads, a fool doesn't want to face facts, because fools love to deceive themselves.

Always get proof when things happen, be patient until things are fixed. The Lord will help if you learn to listen and look for it.

Common sense in a nutshell, is to "Do for others as you would have them do for you."

To stay foolish is to be blind and closed. The wrong image.

Chapter 18

POWER OF THE TONGUE

Somewhere back in eternity's past, God the supreme being of this visible universe decided to make someone like Himself. That would be humankind. According to Genesis in the Bible.

The Designer and Creator gave us a unique gift. It is the ability to speak and talk with God and each other. Not just to make sounds like other creatures but to also know languages, choose our own words and speak them out at will.

With words, all mankind can have a unity of purpose to accomplish goals and tasks.

Words are carriers of spiritual power as well, for good or evil, for blessing or cursing. The miracle book states, "Death and life are in the power of the tongue." (Proverbs 18:21) (KJV)

Man's unique ability to choose and speak words has become a key factor in the development of the human race. When people speak, they are releasing and exposing their inner invisible value system and character. However, since the fall of man into sin and evil, the tongue has become a world of iniquity, an untamed part of the body.

No human can tame the tongue. It is always ready to pour out its deadly poison, blessings and curses. But, we were fashioned to live in such a way that only goodness should flow out of our mouths.

From a young age, my mother taught me and my siblings to watch our mouths, and be quiet to hear and slow to speak, so that we would stay out of trouble.

Our tongues are that small member of our bodies that can, as the book of James chapter 3 states, "Set the course of your future for blessings or curses." (KJV) That is why most parents, teachers and preachers are consistently trying to get people to be positive and watch what they say to others.

What you say is what you really believe and what you really believe in your heart is what will come to pass in your life. The power of words created this universe. The power of words are so great that wars have been fought over miss guided words from leaders. Words can generate fear, hate, love, faith and a call to action.

So, if you desire to become the kind of person that aspires to make a difference in your generation, see to it that you pay close attention to your own words. Your words should be filled with faith, love, kindness, wisdom, inspiration, peace, strength and courage.

Self control means controlling your tongue and emotions. Idle lips are evils mouth piece. These idle lips are filled with strife, gossip, arguing, lies, flattery, boasting, complaining, cursing, pride and negativity.

The way we humans are designed, that which is on the inside of our hearts minds and feelings, will come to the light. The Lord said, "From the fullness of your heart, your mouth will speak." (Matthews 12:34) (KJV)

"A man heart determines his speech." (Matthews 12:34) (TLB)

This is how you can know for yourself what is hidden on the inside of you. Good of evil, light or darkness. Guard your heart and tongue from speaking negative things. **Get more of God's good words inside of you. Foolish and idle talk must be stopped. For you to be greater and more like our Maker.**

You can never be a person of power in God's image and likeness without the transformation of your heart and the taming of your tongue.

Victory in life is God's gift to all of us. From the time we were little children, our dream of achievement is an inborn desire. When parents or teachers acknowledge any accomplishments of a child, this makes them feel very happy and fulfilled. But, children experience sadness when they are disapproved.

The Great Designer of life engineered success and victory into all creation and then placed humankind over all creation to rule. Why then would God limit people and infest us with the virus of failure, poverty and defeat? NO! That is not God's doing, but sin, evil and the wrong identity. God gives all of us power, gifts and abilities and also talents because He desires the human race, to be greater than ourselves.

With God's word in our mouths and actions we become powerful and creative like Him. To do good!

It is written, "Man shall not live by bread alone but by every word that proceeds out of the mouth of the Lord." (Matthews 4:4) (KJV) If you look into God's truths, the Bible every day, you will see and hear Him and then you will be transformed into His image of love as you do what the Lord says.

It was not until man's first parents Adam and Eve chose evil. That evil entered the picture. In the beginning words became twisted and perverted. So now we must be trained by God's Holy Spirit and Word to correct our miss guided words and speak in line with God's will.

Do not be snared by the words of your own mouth, or let other's words stop, hinder or limit you in any way from having good and God's best in your life. Remember good and evil are spiritual forces. I decided within myself to choose the good and watch over the words of my mouth.

Always remember, what you say and believe in your heart is what you will be manifesting.

If you believe in your heart that the Lord will help you He will, that's it. His promises are, "Ask and you will be given, seeking and you will find, and knock and the door will be opened!" (Matthews 7:7) (TLB)

Whatever Jesus Christ says, Believe it, Say it, Do it!

When you were younger did you speak and believe yourself to where you are right now? Have you created crimes of the tongue that kill steal and destroy your future? If you are not satisfied, change it, tools are in God's Book study it.

The designer has built into life's order, the way things are to be. So if your life is surrounded by error, lack, fear or doubt, you are going the wrong way, stop, and change direction. Go God's way!

Read Matthew, Mark, Luke and John to find out the correct use of the tongue and words.

This is what Jesus did:

1. He spoke to the wind, and it obeyed Him.
2. He spoke to the raging sea and it had peace.
3. He spoke to the lost, and they got saved without cost.

4. He spoke to the devils and they obeyed Him on every level.
5. He spoke to the dead and they arose to life instead.
6. He spoke the truth, because with Him lies had no use.
7. He spoke of love, because he was the Lord from above.

Yes, your words will always stand, when they are in line with the Master's plan.

Chapter 19

THE POWER OF AGREEMENT

<u>The power of agreement = unity</u>

What does it mean to agree? How important is it to be agreeable or to have unity and oneness?

To agree simply means, to hit the same note. To sound together as in harmony, or to have the same focus or the same mindset. Agreement is doing something in line with the will, goals, plans or purpose of others.

The opposite picture makes the meaning of agreement even clearer. Division, strife, confusion, chaos, is only the symptoms of lack of agreement and unity.

To produce unity, it is necessary to have at least two or more people come together around a vision or a plan of action.

How is this accomplished?

1. Create an atmosphere of oneness, speaking words of honor and respect towards others.
2. Have a strong drive to produce a good and a successful result.
3. Having the same mental focus, motives and intentions.
4. Willing to yield to others to produce a greater good.

Here is the challenge, even if the mouth of a person is speaking correct words; they can still be division within that individual. That type of person will display double mindedness if they don't really believe what they say. So, in order to have power to accomplish anything you cannot be divided within yourself, all doubt must be removed.

The Good Book says, "How can two walk together except they agree?" (Amos 3:3) (KJV) If a person is a rebel they will not agree because rebels are against good, and against authority.

The power of agreement is vital because, for instance it helps people produce results. In the court of law it takes at least two witnesses to convict a person of guilt in some crimes. One strong person can prevail over one weaker person, but it is much harder against two in an attack. Someone may have trouble lifting heavy objects but with two people it's much easier to lift heavy objects.

This chapter's focus is to make sure that you are in agreement and in order with God's will and purpose for your life. Making sure that you know the importance of maintaining agreement with God's image, and God's identity for you.

Using the example of a soldier can make the concept of agreement even clearer. A person desiring to be a soldier has to be trained in the ways of the war. This requires practice, drills, discipline, and sacrifice to form a military combat state of mind.

Soldiers have to learn to take orders without questions, also learning the importance of being apart of a unit.

A good soldier must learn mental toughness and survival skills. The ultimate goal is to make these soldiers function as one with one purpose.

Oneness creates motion, force, productivity. In a team sport it is a given, that the team with the most valuable players, and the team that plays great together will not only win games but will probably win the championship.

The key ingredients here, is to always maintain unity, agreements coupled with discipline, hard work and skill.

In the business world as in the sports world we often hear this word spoken, focus; so what is focus?

Focus is displayed when there is unity of purpose within someone being. There heart mind and body, is lined up to accomplish something.

Integrity is a type of focus, where your values are lined up within you to accomplish good and honest behavior.

The designer is the most powerful being that exists; He is all knowing and seeing. To be one with the Lord of heaven and earth is our greatest privilege and honor. The focus of God's Word is for us to know Him and be like Him. So let us think about this for a second, whose image do you reflect? When you look in the mirror of your soul, and stare at yourself. Do you like what you see? Do you need a spiritual makeover? A spiritual transformation? If you don't like what you see get your God identity back, and take off those fake robes of superiority and or insecurities that you wear. Just be who God says, who-you-are to be.

The Bible says, "One can put 1000 to flight and two put 10,000 to flight." (Deuteronomy 32:30) (KJV)

This verse is reflecting the power of agreement in war, when God is with the believers against spiritual enemies. Two believers are many times stronger and greater than one.

The Bible is the Lord's training manual, for those he has called and chosen to be in His army of faith and love. His super heroes with power to do good with His authority, remember God is your back up!

So when you check your life's focus, are you lost in the world that is perishing, forever chasing fun and excitement? Or are you in God's kingdom that will never end, where you can find eternal life.

It is time for you to flip the switch and turn on the light. This invitation is for believers and unbelievers. Say yes to Jesus and His ways, get into agreement with Him.

It is time to get on the winning team; the championship has already been won. We are in a world that simply looks at people as dollar signs pushing their bad habits 24 hours a day.

Now, what turns you on the most and captures your time and attention is where your heart is. We must put the Lord, the Source first in our lives. It is His universe that we are enjoying, this is His playground not ours. We should put His business before ours, His character and image before our pleasures and desires do you agree?

Yes, it is plain to see in the news, that just about anyone rich or poor, famous or unknown can crash and fall into a mountain of troubles.

Here is my poetry for unity with God and man.

1. Live inside outward for you.
2. What is beyond visible live that too.
3. Always look from the Lord's point of view.
4. To see further and brand-new.
5. Look up, not down to find your way.

6. Be light not darkness every day.
7. God's image and likeness, you must choose.
8. The spirit over the flesh must rule.
9. Love conquers hate when you pray.
10. Enjoy your life with others in a good way.
11. Having faith in God will silence all your fears.
12. Love truth, not lies in your ears.
13. Agreement over division is life, reject strife.
14. Invite Christ into your life, He knows what's right.
15. Let God's strength, defeat your weak living.
16. And be someone's friend with your giving.
17. Agree with God's Word to be free, then He will give you the victory with unity.

Chapter 20

OBEDIENCE

"To whom you yield yourselves servant to obey, their servant you are to whom you obey." (Romans 6:16) (KJV)

Webster's dictionary defines obedience as devotion, loyalty, faithfulness, to yield, to serve, to comply, to submit to authority.

These words carry the key ingredients for us to be true over-comers and victorious in life. This section on obedience is a field of gold, that I hope will help to change and transform you forever.

"If you be willing and obedient, you will eat the good of the land but if you refuse and rebel, you shall be destroyed." (Isaiah 1:19, 20) (KJV)

These words are from the Lord and they are the blueprint of conduct, that we should tailor into our every situation. We must be willing and obedient. A doer with a good attitude to experience real success. This scripture does not just say to obey, but to be willing to obey.

Question; do you have a willing heart? A sincere humble heart? What I am saying, do not be a half hearted worker, self-serving and self willed. **Always do your very best, be excellent at whatever you do, and make God, your Maker, smile.**

The Lord gives us every ability we need to succeed. However, "Rebellion is as bad as the sin of witchcraft, and stubbornness is as bad as worshipping idols." (1 Samuel 15:22, 23) (TLB)

A life of obedience is connected to the power of humility. The more prideful or selfish a person is, they will have conflicts and disputes in everything. Also the Bible states, "God exalts the humble." (1 Peter 5:6) (KJV)

To be in authority, one must learn to submit to authority. There is always going to be people over people over people, telling you what to do.

Respectful obedience takes strength not weakness.

Employers have bosses, teachers have principles, the military and police have superior officers over them. In every arena of life, obedience is needed. These are the check and balance of authority.

People sometimes feel the pressure of doing what they are told by superiors, because of pride. But the smart obedient ones have taken the pressure off themselves, by doing their jobs willfully and cheerfully with their whole heart.

We are to give respect where respect is due. Give honor where honor due. It takes power to have an obedient, humble attitude.

I believe when someone does whatsoever they do to please the Lord first and foremost, that is a great reward within itself. Being faithful to your task shows your honesty integrity and character, the right spirit and the right image.

The love of money can be one of the main enemies of an individual operating in obedience. Being overly money minded has an effect to replace the goodwill in your attitude with pride, selfishness and greed.

Materialism can become a person's idol, causing that person to reflect the wrong image of self serving, self-centered and hard to work with. Now, ask yourself at this point; "Are you acting self-made or God-made?" You can't be both.

Money should only be our servant and not our master. Money should only be thought of as a tool, a means to an end. Try thinking of an expensive car as a fancy horse or merely a mode of transportation, that's all it is. When we think right, we see right and do right.

Then people can be free from the pride of self importance and the shame of poverty.

When money is your master, you will become its slave and obey it.

It is the Lord, the Image Maker, who should be your security. Insecure people always worry about how they appear to others. Be secure, look up, because that is where our help comes from.

Fear and insecurity are always the wrong image, the wrong spirit and the wrong fruit.

The Lord says, "Whatever you do in word or deed, eat or drink, do all to the glory of God." (1 Corinthians 10:31) (KJV) That should be your secret to success.

The virtue of obedience will bring power into your life. "God resists the proud, but gives grace to the humble." (James 4:6) (KJV) "Let every soul be subject to the higher power, for there is no power but of God, the powers that be are ordained of God." (Romans 13:1) (KJV)

The Lord is not saying that we must obey the laws in authority if they are in error against Gods Word. However, our obedience is to God's ways of dealing with all circumstances.

It is very important that we watch how we talk against leaders in government, especially if we are not praying for them. When we fail to show respect and honor, we are in rebellion against God's order.

Sometime ago there was an academy award winning film, back in the 80s called "Chariots of Fire." The movie was based on a true story of a Cambridge University student named Eric Liddell, in England that run track and field.

Eric ran twice as fast as all of the other runners. The other athletes would train hard to prepare to beat this guy, but Eric kept right on winning the races.

As the story goes, when asked by news reporters, "You have such an odd untrained style of running, why do you think you are so fast?" He replied, "When I run, **I want to make God smile, I want to please the Lord because he gave me this gift. God made me fast I run for His pleasure!**"

"To Win is to Honor Him!" (KE)

Our Creator knows us better than we know ourselves, we cannot even imagine what mankind would be if we would totally yield to Him.

Just do what you do, to put a smile on God's face, and see what He does in return for you and through you.

The designer is the one that can truly fix the broken hearted and help us to be the best we can be.

This track and field runner had the heart of a champion. So, likewise if we would relax and trust and obey the Lord's will, found in His book. We too will bring God pleasure and feel the success of doing everything for His glory.

It is written, "Man was made in God's image and likeness." I need not to try to explain what all of that means, because we only know in part. But, what I do know is this, everything God has made was good and very good before the fall. So it is a good thing to love God, serve Him and love people also.

There has to be order in society, to obey orders and those in authority in line with the Word of God is to fight against evil. When good people do nothing, evil prospers.

If everyone did what was right in their own eyes, crimes would be rampant in every home. Revenge would be the norm. People would simply take matters into their own hands, and the result would be **no love, no laws, and no order.**

To put it bluntly, obedience helps us all, to keep the dogs off our butts, so to speak. Obedience is the path to your success.

We start life as babies needing to be taught and educated, learning right from wrong, good from evil, etc.

So if we listen and obey our parents and teachers and not rebel, we will feast on the good life.

But, if we refuse here comes trouble. Do not be like concrete, mixed up and permanently set. Obedience is power that will put you on top. It signals you out of the crowd, as one who can be trusted, a winner, a leader, a helper, a true friend. When people are respectful and understanding, they tend to do things with a certain level of quality. This ingredient of obedience will make you more attractive to be put in authority.

Could you imagine voters electing a president that did not respect others or did not care about the laws? Voters look for quality of faithfulness, willing to yield, intelligence, loyalty, honesty, hard work and a servant's heart.

This book is about you the reader becoming and growing into the right image. The image and likeness of God Almighty. God's spirit and character is our destiny. He is seeking worshippers and a family.

WARNING! WARNING! RED FLAGS!

Disobedience will only bring punishment and destruction.

"It is written, the wrath of God comes on the children of disobedience." (Colossians 3:6) (KJV)

"Remember to whom you yield to obey their servant or slave, you are, good or evil."

At first I refused God's Word and rejected his image, but I was defenseless against my Savior's love and my mother's prayers and wisdom.

When I let God's high values and unseen gifts inside of me flow freely and joyfully they lead me upward not downward. It is as simple as this, **take a look inside God's Book and see if you fit!**

Are you wearing Christ greatness? Or are you letting the devil wear you out?

At the end of life's journey, the question will be obvious; did you follow the chain of command from above? And were you willing and obedient to give love? If your answer is yes, and you did not rebel.

Then you will hear the #1 Image Maker say, "Well done my good and faithful servant." (Mission accomplished!)

Chapter 21

THE END OR THE BEGINNING

Our newsstands, movies, TV shows, internet sites and music videos are filled with lewd and obscene images. The human appetite and cravings for new thrills seem to be at an all time high. So many celebrity news shows feeding consumers minute by minute, garbage on these celebrity meltdowns, is almost nauseating.

Why does it seem like humanity is sinking lower and lower into evil as time goes on? I believe there is an invisible line being drawn between the good and the evil, the light and the darkness, so don't be caught on the wrong side of the line my friend.

It's time to go another way! Change direction, turn around! I heard a preacher say it like this, repent, and this was his spin, re-(go back to the) pent (the top). Penthouse!! God's class!

What he was expressing to me, was go back to the Lord's original image, purpose and position for mankind. Take back your stolen identity. Go back to the place of power, purity, with our first love, God!

This is the place where all things are possible with the Lord's help. The place where we love to do God's will. The place where we are dressed and suited in His greatness, created for success. Pleasing Him in everything we do and say.

It's not enough to just feel sorry and remorse for our disobedience and sins. We must step out of darkness into His light, and be a new creation. People fashioned like God, modeling His lifestyle, boldly reflecting His goodness. In this world for all to see.

The Lord's arms are open wide; He has forgiven all of our sins, if we believe and receive forgiveness.

"Love is looking for love today, send yours in right away." Stevie Wonder

God is seeking you, to give you His eternal life and His everything. No lie! No fairy tale.

Don't say no! Do not close the door in God's face; He wants to make you His child of love. Do you feel empty, weak, undernourished, so to speak, on the inside? Well God's help is right here, right now, calling you, it's your choice to answer. **Say YES to Jesus in your heart!**

How beautiful the loving parents, who cuddle their little ones tenderly, with loving care. And as the child grows, they provide food, clothing security and development. Why? Because it is their love and responsibility to do so. When you become a member of God's family, the question is will God the Almighty do any less than two imperfect parents? Yes! He will! Care for you! And me!

My intention in this book is simply to inspire and put a fire in you, to be bold and to step out of the box of limitations, and let God be God in you, today. This universe is bigger than mans imagination. Someone

all powerful created it, so stop lying to yourself about that... recognize him.

When we see God, who is invisible in a visible world, we become His witnesses. God's family, God's lovers.

Now is the time, and this is the day, to receive the light of truth, about what's really going on in this world.

This is how to be transformed from a caterpillar to a soaring eagle. We will be held responsible for all the gifts, talents and power we use, and for the free will choices we make daily.

Remember, everyday gives all of us another chance to get it right, and step into the light. Christ's sacrifice of His life on the cross was bold and very courageous, open for all to see. So you and I must be bold and very courageous, with His lifestyle, for all to see. Jesus said, "I will be ashamed of all who is ashamed of me."
(Luke 9:26) (TLB)

To be in God's family of love, we must be born into it, or born again into it. God's Holy Spirit gives us this new life. It has to be a free will choice. God, our Maker, isn't looking for robots, clones or programmed people.

The Father of heaven and earth is seeking sons and daughters that will follow Him and model Him. Like I stated before, "If you are willing and obedient, you shall be blessed by God, but if you refuse and rebel, you shall perish."

"Hell is licking its lips in anticipation of the delicious morsel of lost souls." (Isaiah 5:14) (TLB)

"Where the word of a king is, there is great power!" (Ecclesiastes 8:4) (TLB)

No Word of God is void of power! Believe it! Reverence it! Trust it!

The miracle book says, "If you can believe, all things are possible to those who believe." (Mark 9:23) (KJV) Authority has to be backed by power, just as police are backed by local and state government, courts, laws and guns.

It is the same in the courts of heaven; we are backed up by God Himself.

Believers are given weapons that are not physical but mighty through God to the pulling down of strong holds. (2 Corinthians 10:4) (KJV)

Also, Christ said, "All power in heaven and earth is given to me." (Matthews 28:18) (KJV)

These words say it all. Christ is the Word of God, The Source, The Gift Giver, The Holy One. King of kings and Lord of lords.

Super means: above, over, higher, superior, endowed with power beyond the natural.

Hero means: champion, conqueror, warrior, saint, valiant, fearless, brave, and courageous.

Now everyone has their favorite superhero. Some love Superman, Spiderman or Wonder Woman, just to name a few. These heroes are celebrated because they do wonderful deeds, fight the bad guys, and rescue people from perishing. While upholding truth and justice.

My all time number one Super Hero is Jesus Christ, The Messiah, and The Son of God. He did many real historically documented, supernatural things. He healed sick and broken hearted people, raised people from the dead, and cast out evil spirits with a Word. He saves the lost and sets captives free from spiritual darkness, and ignorance.

But this story of Christ wasn't a movie or a marvel comic book depiction of fictional characters. He is The Lord from Heaven, The #1 Image Maker and the soon to return, King of the Universe.

The earth is only a part and start of the journey. The Image Maker is calling for you and I to take the journey of life with Him and become the transformed super heroes of faith to our generation.

"So let us foolproof out lives with God's Word, so that we won't be the fools and miss heaven." Pastor Mel Ayres- In His Presence Church.

ABOUT THE AUTHOR

Keith E. Echols is a teacher national published author, CEO of The Mark Rich Agency and media executive.

His mission as an author is to impact, teach and inspire divine excellence in people.

The #1 Image Maker book is a road map, a runway for take off and GPS to guide readers to the ultimate and absolute question of life. Why are we here? Why do we exist? Where did we come from? And why do we have such intelligence, talents and abilities that separate us from the animal kingdom, producing computers, micro-chips satellites and discovering quantum physics etc.

Mr. Echols goal in the writing of The #1 Image Maker is to deliver a powerful message for all of us, in school at home, at work or at play, young and old, rich or poor or in between to take back your stolen identity and discover The Image Maker. His great purpose for mankind before time runs out on this Great Planet Earth, is his inspired message.

Printed in the United States
By Bookmasters